FUNCLE

NOTEBOOK

FUNCLE
NOTEBOOK

FUNCLE

NOTEBOOK

FUNCLE
NOTEBOOK

FUNCLE
NOTEBOOK

FUNCLE
NOTEBOOK

FUNCLE
NOTEBOOK

FUNCLE

NOTEBOOK

FUNCLE NOTEBOOK

FUNCLE
NOTEBOOK

# FUNCLE NOTEBOOK

FUNCLE
NOTEBOOK

FUNCLE

NOTEBOOK

FUNCLE
NOTEBOOK

FUNCLE
NOTEBOOK

FUNCLE
NOTEBOOK

FUNCLE
NOTEBOOK

FUNCLE
NOTEBOOK

FUNCLE

NOTEBOOK

FUNCLE NOTEBOOK

FUNCLE NOTEBOOK

FUNCLE

NOTEBOOK

FUNCLE

NOTEBOOK

FUNCLE

NOTEBOOK

FUNCLE
NOTEBOOK

FUNCLE

NOTEBOOK

FUNCLE

NOTEBOOK

FUNCLE
NOTEBOOK

FUNCLE
NOTEBOOK

FUNCLE

NOTEBOOK

FUNCLE
NOTEBOOK

FUNCLE
NOTEBOOK

FUNCLE
NOTEBOOK

FUNCLE
NOTEBOOK

FUNCLE NOTEBOOK

FUNCLE

NOTEBOOK

FUNCLE
NOTEBOOK

FUNCLE NOTEBOOK

FUNCLE

NOTEBOOK

FUNCLE
NOTEBOOK

FUNCLE
NOTEBOOK

FUNCLE
NOTEBOOK

FUNCLE

NOTEBOOK

FUNCLE
NOTEBOOK

FUNCLE
NOTEBOOK

FUNCLE NOTEBOOK

FUNCLE
NOTEBOOK

FUNCLE
NOTEBOOK

FUNCLE
NOTEBOOK

FUNCLE
NOTEBOOK

FUNCLE
NOTEBOOK

FUNCLE
NOTEBOOK

FUNCLE

NOTEBOOK

FUNCLE

NOTEBOOK

FUNCLE

NOTEBOOK

FUNCLE

NOTEBOOK

FUNCLE
NOTEBOOK

FUNCLE
NOTEBOOK

FUNCLE
NOTEBOOK

FUNCLE NOTEBOOK

FUNCLE

NOTEBOOK

FUNCLE NOTEBOOK

FUNCLE
NOTEBOOK

FUNCLE
NOTEBOOK

FUNCLE

NOTEBOOK

FUNCLE
NOTEBOOK

FUNCLE

NOTEBOOK

# FUNCLE NOTEBOOK

FUNCLE

NOTEBOOK

FUNCLE
NOTEBOOK

FUNCLE

NOTEBOOK

FUNCLE
NOTEBOOK

FUNCLE NOTEBOOK

FUNCLE NOTEBOOK

FUNCLE
NOTEBOOK

FUNCLE
NOTEBOOK

FUNCLE NOTEBOOK

FUNCLE NOTEBOOK

FUNCLE
NOTEBOOK

FUNCLE

NOTEBOOK

FUNCLE

NOTEBOOK

FUNCLE NOTEBOOK

FUNCLE NOTEBOOK

www.ingramcontent.com/pod-product-compliance
Lightning Source LLC
LaVergne TN
LVHW060328080526
838202LV00053B/4441
*9783347160491*